MW00795502

My First Animal Library

Wildebeests

by Penelope S. Nelson

Bullfrog Books

Ideas for Parents and Teachers

Bullfrog Books let children practice reading informational text at the earliest reading levels. Repetition, familiar words, and photo labels support early readers.

Before Reading

- Discuss the cover photo. What does it tell them?
- Look at the picture glossary together. Read and discuss the words.

Read the Book

- "Walk" through the book and look at the photos. Let the child ask questions. Point out the photo labels.
- Read the book to the child, or have him or her read independently.

After Reading

- Prompt the child to think more. Ask: Did you know about wildebeests before reading this book? What more would you like to learn about them after reading it?

Bullfrog Books are published by Jump!
5357 Penn Avenue South
Minneapolis, MN 55419
www.jumplibrary.com

Library of Congress Cataloging-in-Publication Data

Names: Nelson, Penelope, 1994– author.
Title: Wildebeests / by Penelope S. Nelson.
Description: Bullfrog books edition.
Minneapolis, MN : Jump!, Inc., [2020]
Series: My first animal library
Audience: Age 5–8. | Audience: K to Grade 3.
Includes index.
Identifiers: LCCN 2018040306 (print)
LCCN 2018041698 (ebook)
ISBN 9781641285650 (ebook)
ISBN 9781641285643 (hardcover : alk. paper)
Subjects: LCSH: Gnus—Juvenile literature.
Classification: LCC QL737.U53 (ebook)
LCC QL737.U53 N47 2020 (print)
DDC 599.64/59—dc23
LC record available at https://lccn.loc.gov/2018040306

Editor: Jenna Trnka
Designer: Jenna Casura

Photo Credits: Aberson/iStock, cover; Lois GoBe/Shutterstock, 1; Vladimir Wrangel/Shutterstock, 3; GUDKOV ANDREY/Shutterstock, 4, 23bl; Ulrich Doering/Alamy, 5; Monique D/Shutterstock, 6–7, 23tr; KenCanning/iStock, 8–9; Travel Stock/Shutterstock, 10; pilesasmiles/iStock, 11; Paul Souders/Getty, 12–13, 23br; SUE GOULD/Shutterstock, 14; Pyty/Shutterstock, 15; LeonP/Shutterstock, 16–17; Ariadne Van Zandbergen/Alamy, 18–19, 23tl; imageBROKER/Alamy, 20–21; Eric Isselee/Shutterstock, 22; GlobalP/iStock, 24.

Printed in the United States of America at Corporate Graphics in North Mankato, Minnesota.

Table of Contents

On the Move

It is spring.

Wildebeests migrate.

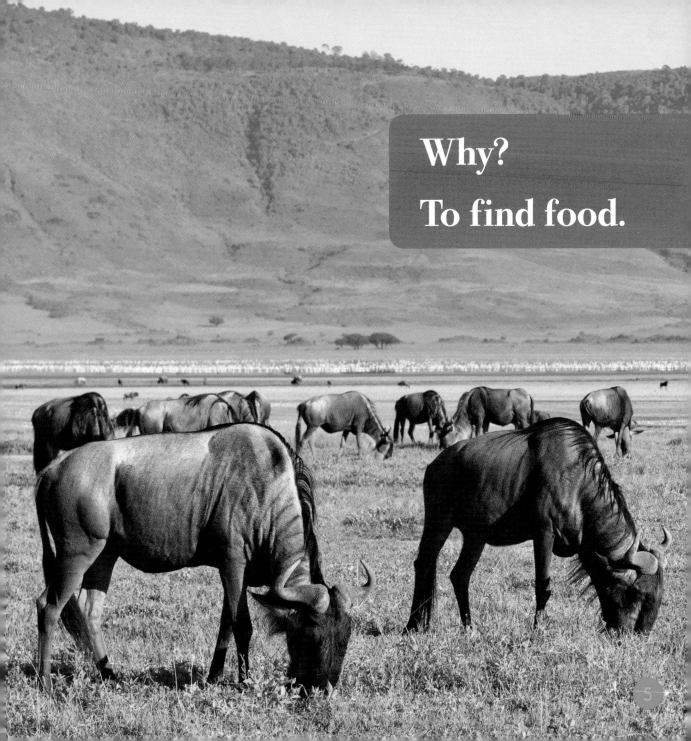

Why?

To find food.

5

herd

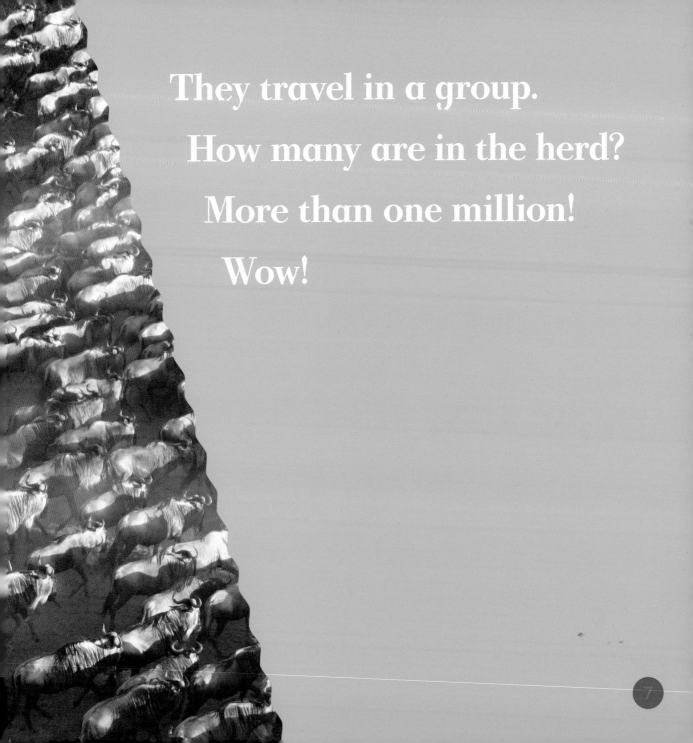

They travel in a group.

How many are in the herd?

More than one million!

Wow!

The herd goes far.
It even crosses rivers.
Cool!

river

horns

They have horns.
They point up.

10

What are they for?

Fighting.

They fight each other.

lion

They fight predators, too.

Like what?

Lions. Hyenas.
Crocodiles.

stripe

A wildebeest is hairy.
It has stripes.

mane

beard

What else?

A mane and beard.

They grow big.

How much does one weigh?

As much as a car!

calf

A mom has one calf.
The calf walks right away.

Then it runs!

It keeps up
with the herd.

Parts of a Wildebeest

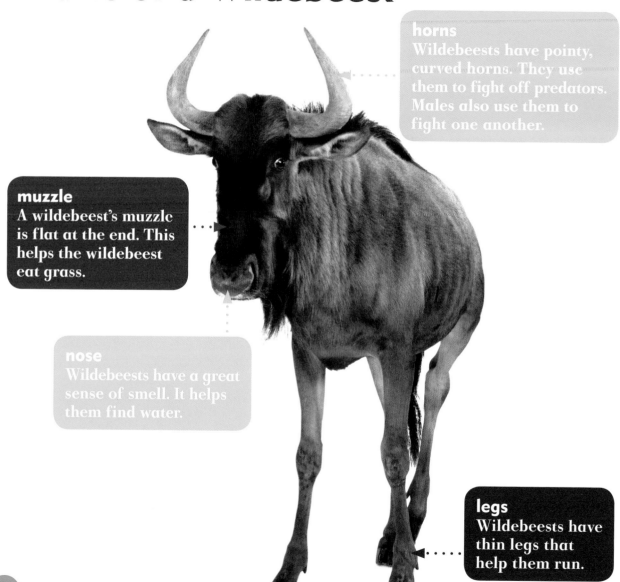

horns
Wildebeests have pointy, curved horns. They use them to fight off predators. Males also use them to fight one another.

muzzle
A wildebeest's muzzle is flat at the end. This helps the wildebeest eat grass.

nose
Wildebeests have a great sense of smell. It helps them find water.

legs
Wildebeests have thin legs that help them run.

Picture Glossary

calf
A young wildebeest.

herd
A group of wildebeests.

migrate
To move from one area
to another at a certain
time of year.

predators
Animals that hunt other
animals for food.

Index

To Learn More

Finding more information is as easy as 1, 2, 3.

❶ Go to www.factsurfer.com

❷ Enter "wildebeests" into the search box.

❸ Click the "Surf" button to see a list of websites.